As Quiet As A MOUSE

'As Quiet As A Mouse'
An original concept by Karen Owen
© Karen Owen

Illustrated by Evgenia Golubeva

Published by MAVERICK ARTS PUBLISHING LTD
Studio 3A, City Business Centre, 6 Brighton Road,
Horsham, West Sussex, RH13 5BB
© Maverick Arts Publishing Limited June 2016
+44 (0)1403 256941

A CIP catalogue record for this book is available at the British Library.

ISBN 978-1-84886-226-5

www.maverickbooks.co.uk

This book is rated as: Turquoise Band
The original picture book text for this story has been modified by the author to be an early reader.

As Quiet As A Mouse

written by **Karen Owen**

illustrated by **Evgenia Golubeva**

Edgar loved his new baby sister.

Mabel was small and cute and liked sleeping. But Edgar was so noisy he kept waking her up.

"Edgar! You sound like a whole herd of elephants, not just one little elephant!" said Mum.

"Sorry," said Edgar.

"Wahhhh!" said Mabel.

Edgar tried to be quiet. He tiptoed.

He crawled. He put on his soft slippers.

But then....

"Edgar!" said Mum. "You need to be as quiet as a mouse!"

"Why are you looking so sad?"

asked Edgar's friend, Ruby.

Edgar told her about his noisy problem.

"I've got an idea!" Ruby said.

So Edgar followed Ruby...

...all the way to Mouse School.

"Edgar wants to be as quiet as a mouse," Ruby told Mr Cheddar, the Head Mouse.

"How can an elephant be as quiet as a mouse?" asked Mr Cheddar.

"Please let me try," said Edgar.

"You'll have to pass the Quiet Mouse Test," said Mr Cheddar.

Edgar bounced up and down VERY noisily.

"Can we start straight away please?"

"Walk across the stage," said Mr Cheddar.

"Not like that! Like this!" said Mr Cheddar.

He walked quietly across the stage.

So did the little mice.

Edgar couldn't hear them at all!

"Oh dear! I'll never be that quiet,"

he thought.

Mr Cheddar tried hard to teach Edgar to walk...

And tiptoe. And dance.

Finally, it was time to take the Quiet Mouse Test.

Edgar and his friends walked and tiptoed and danced. The audience clapped quietly.

Mr Cheddar beamed. "I am pleased to announce that Edgar is the first elephant who is as quiet as a mouse," he said.

Edgar was so proud he swished his trunk...

very quietly, of course.

"Well done to all of our quiet winners...

Now it's party time!" said Mr Cheddar.

"Hurray!" The mice cheered and rushed to eat all the party food.

"Shhhh!" whispered Edgar's mum.

But she was too late…

"Wahhhh!" cried Mabel.

Mum covered up her ears. "You sound like…"

"A herd of ELEPHANTS!"

Quiz

1. What does Edgar put on his feet to try to be quiet?
a) Thick socks
b) Pillows
c) Soft slippers

2. What is Ruby's teacher called?
a) Mr Cheddar
b) Mr Cheese
c) Mr Edam

3. Why is Edgar sad?
a) He wants to be quiet
b) He does not like his new sister
c) He wants to be a mouse

4. What test does Edgar have to take?
a) As Silent As A Snake test
b) As Quiet As A Mouse test
c) The Tiptoe test

5. What party food is there?
a) Cheese and bananas
b) Cheese and bread
c) Cheese and sausage rolls

Turn over for answers

- Light Pink
- Dark Pink
- Red (End of Yr R)
- Yellow
- Blue
- Green
- Orange
- Turquoise (End of Yr 1)
- Purple
- Gold
- White (End of Yr 2)
- Lime

Book Bands for Guided Reading

The Institute of Education book banding system is made up of twelve colours, which reflect the level of reading difficulty. The bands are assigned by taking into account the content, the language style, the layout and phonics.

Children learn at different speeds but the colour chart shows the levels of progression with the national expectation shown in brackets. To learn more visit the IoE website: www.ioe.ac.uk.

Maverick early readers have been adapted from the original picture books so that children can make the essential transition from listener to reader. All of these books have been book banded for guided reading to the industry standard and edited by a leading educational consultant.

Quiz Answers: 1c, 2a, 3a, 4b, 5a